paint MAGIC

D1307058

NORTH LIGHT BOOKS
CINCINNATI, OH

Visit our Web site at www.artistsnetwork.com for information on more resources for artists.

04 03 02 01 00   5 4 3 2 1

The catalog record for this book is available from the U.S. Library of Congress.

ISBN 1-58180-231-5

American Editor: Diane Ridley Schmitz
Editorial Production Manager: Kathi Howard
Production Supervisor: Kristen Heller
American Designer: Kevin Martin
Studio Manager: Ruth Preston

Contents

All About Paints
4

All About Brushes
5

Rocket Launch!
6

Heavy Hedgehogs
9

How to Make Waves
10

Wild Strawberries
12

Manatee Magic
15

Color Combing
16

Snowy Robin
18

Brilliant Bags!
21

All About Blow Pens
22

Frog Frolics
24

Paint a Night Owl
27

Tile Style
29

A Fry Up!
30

The Loch Ness Monster
32

Straw Blowing Fun
35

Alien Alert
38

All About Finger Painting
41

Finger Printing
42

Thumbprint Giftwrap!
43

Incr-edible Landscape
44

Funky Pharaoh
47

Bright Butterfly
50

Ice Cream Dream!
53

Go Dotty!
56

All About Inks
59

Snazzy Snake
60

Salty Citrus
63

All about... PAINTS

There are lots of different types of paints, such as oils and acrylics. However, the two that you are most likely to use are watercolors and poster paints.

Poster paints

Poster paints are like thick watercolors and the most expensive kind is called gouache (say gwarsh). White is added to all poster paint colors, which makes them thicker than watercolors and less transparent. This also makes them duller than watercolors. Poster paints are easy to spread thickly and are quick drying. They are good for painting on to lots of different surfaces, like cardboard and papier-mâché.

Watercolors

Watercolor paints are made of powders called pigments which come from such things as plants, earth and rocks. These are mixed with plant gum which binds the paint together. There are two types of watercolors: dry cakes of paint you rub with a wet brush, and tubes of thick paint. For beginners, dry watercolors are easiest to use. You can use special watercolor paper and 'stretch' it first by wetting it and taping it to a board to dry. Then it won't wrinkle when the paint is applied.

Top tips!

Watercolor know-how

- Using more water on your brush will make your colors lighter.
- Light colored watercolors won't cover darker colors, so use your light colors first.
- Gently apply thin layers of paint to build up the colors.
- Leave the paper blank for the areas that should be white.

Poster paint know-how

- Start painting with the dark colors and finish with the light ones.
- Don't use shiny paper or the paint will slide off the surface.
- Your paper should be quite thick or it will wrinkle up under the wet paint.

All about... BRUSHES

Paintbrushes come in various shapes and sizes. Some have soft bristles, for watercolor paints, and others have stiffer bristles, for oil and acrylic paints. Sets of nylon brushes are cheaper, and are a good idea when you are learning to paint.

Size it up!

The number stamped on your paintbrush handle will tell you how thick the brush is. **000** is the smallest size you can buy and number **14** is one of the biggest.

Round brushes have bristles that get longer in the middle and form a point.

Flat brushes have quite a wide brush head and the tips of the bristles are cut completely straight.

Bristle facts

Professional artists use different types of brushes for different jobs.

● Round brushes are good for painting narrow lines and dots, and adding details.

● Flat brushes are better for larger areas of color and for blending colors.

● The best watercolor brushes have sable bristles – artists use them because they last a long time and keep their shape.

● The best brushes for oils and acrylics are made from hog bristle.

To start painting, you will need only three round paintbrushes: thin (size 3-4), medium (size 7-8) and thick (size 12-14). Nylon brushes are fine. You can paint details, fill in small shapes, and cover large areas with just these three sizes.

Make your own brush holder

Cardboard tubes make great paintbrush holders. Use an empty snack container, which may already have a metal bottom, or tape a disc of thick card to the bottom of an open tube. Ask an adult to cut it to size if it's too tall, then cover it with jazzy wrapping paper. Put marbles in the tube to weigh down the base, then your holder won't fall over.

FUN FACTS Sable brushes come from the pine marten, a small, furry animal that is like a weasel. Pine martens are expert tree climbers. They leap from branch to branch, using their tails like parachutes!

Color class

WET PAPER ✓
PAINTING

Rocket launch!

We have lift-off! Learn how to make your own rocket picture, using splotches of paint on wet paper.

Dab a blob of paint on to wet paper and see what happens – the color spreads out into a brilliant blurry pattern! Keep adding blobs and you can paint a whole picture – without brushstrokes!

● Tape your paper to a piece of cardboard before you start – this stops it wrinkling as the paint dries.

● Make sure the paper is wet all over before you dab on the paint.

● Experiment first – try different colors and brushes.

What you need:

★ Masking tape
★ 2 sheets of thick white paper
★ Lightweight cardboard, larger than your paper
★ Poster paints in turquoise, blue, dark orange and bright orange
★ 4 saucers
★ Pencil
★ Large paintbrushes
★ Jar of water
★ Eraser
★ Scissors
★ Crayons in red, yellow, black and white
★ White glue

ha ha!
How does a happy rocket feel?
over the moon!

FUN FACTS

● Rockets have powerful engines that push them through the sky at 24,850 miles per hour - that's over 32 times faster than the speed of sound (760 miles per hour). Rockets travel this fast so they can break out of the earth's gravity.

● In 1961 the Russian Yuri Alekseyivich Gagarin became the first person to successfully fly in space. Four years later, in 1965, another Russian, Alexei Leonov, took the first steps in space, outside his spacecraft. Then in 1969, Neil Armstrong became the first person to walk on the moon.

1 Tape a sheet of thick paper on to some cardboard. Pour a little turquoise, blue, dark and bright orange paint into separate saucers.

2 Next, draw a rough outline for the smoke and flames. Use light pencil marks so that, when you paint over them later, they don't show through.

3 Using a large brush and clean water, wet the paper all over. Make sure it is still wet when you start to paint the sky, flames and smoke.

4 Dab blobs of turquoise and blue paint above the pencil guideline, to make the sky. Let the colors spread out to make a blurry, cloudy pattern.

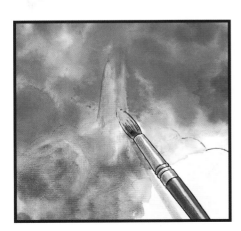

5 Dab on dark and bright orange paint for smoke and flames. Paint orange stripes coming out of the rocket. Leave to dry. Erase pencil guidelines.

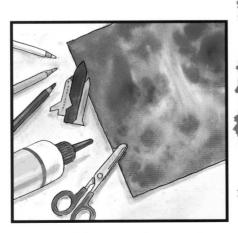

6 On thick paper, draw and cut out a rocket. Color it in with red and yellow crayons. Add details with black and white crayons. Glue the rocket in place.

Quickdraw
...a space shuttle

Start by drawing a long, thin oblong.

Next, draw a smaller oblong on the left. Then add another on the right, overlapping the first oblong.

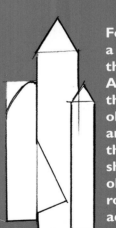

For the rocket, draw a triangle on top of the center oblong. Add a triangle to the top of the oblong on the right, and draw a tail at the bottom. For the shuttle, give the oblong on the left a rounded top and add a wing.

Add details to finish your rocket. Give the shuttle a tail and windows. Draw smoke coming out of the rocket.

7

Doodle paint!

Doodle anything you like with a few blobs of paint on wet paper. When the blobs are dry, add details in crayon, paint or felt-tip pen. Here are just a few ideas…

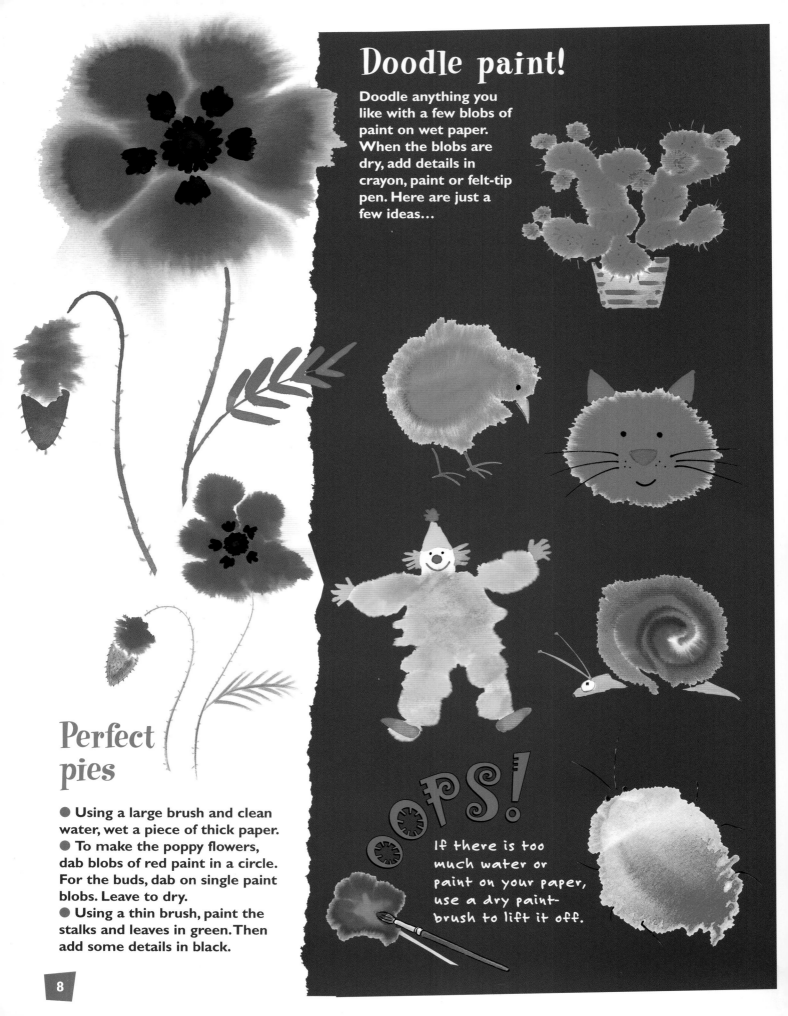

Perfect pies

- Using a large brush and clean water, wet a piece of thick paper.
- To make the poppy flowers, dab blobs of red paint in a circle. For the buds, dab on single paint blobs. Leave to dry.
- Using a thin brush, paint the stalks and leaves in green. Then add some details in black.

OOPS!

If there is too much water or paint on your paper, use a dry paint-brush to lift it off.

Heavy hedgehogs

Stop your papers from blowing away with a perky, pebble paperweight!

What you need:
★ Clean, smooth, large pebble with a flat bottom ★ Pencil ★ Medium and fine paintbrushes ★ Poster paints in dark blue, light blue and pink ★ White glue

1 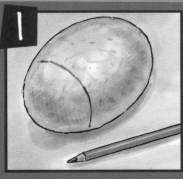 Make sure your pebble is clean. Draw a curved, pencil line on your pebble one third of the way along, to divide the head of the hedgehog from its body.

2  Use a medium paintbrush to paint the body dark blue and the head light blue. Add dark blue spots on the face for the hedgehog's eyes and nose.

3 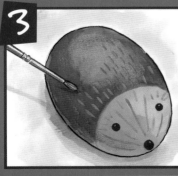 When dry, use a fine paintbrush to paint pink lines on the face. Then, carefully add tiny pink spines all over the body. Let the paint dry.

4  Finally, brush the pebble with a layer of white glue. When it dries, it will become a shiny varnish. Now, make a whole family of pebble paperweights!

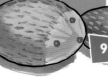

How to make waves

COLORWASH ✓
COLORING ✓
DRAWING ✓

Learn how to make a colorwash and create your own seaside paradise.

What you need:
★ Watercolor paper
★ Lightweight cardboard, larger than your paper
★ Masking tape
★ Watercolor paints in mid blue, white and brown
★ Saucer ★ Jar ★ Ruler
★ Large and thin brushes
★ 2B pencil ★ Eraser
★ Felt-tip pens in green, blue, brown and red

● To mix up paint for the colorwash, fill a jar with clean water, wet a large brush and dab some blue paint on to a saucer. Now, keep adding water to the blue, a little at a time, until the color is fairly light.

● You'll be painting the color-wash on to your paper in one go, so the color gets lighter as you go down the paper and looks just like sea and sky.

STOP! Stretching paper

Before you use a colorwash, you'll have to stretch your paper to stop it wrinkling. Using a large brush, thoroughly wet your paper with water. Lay it on some cardboard, tape it firmly in place and leave to dry.

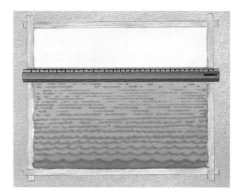

1 First, lightly wet the paper. Starting at the top, brush the wash across the paper from left to right. Leave to dry.

2 Turn the board and paper round. Lightly draw in the horizon with a ruler and pencil. Use felt-tip pens to add waves.

Making waves

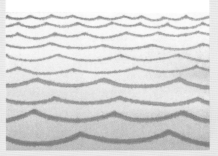

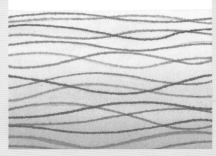

To make waves look further away, draw the lines closer together nearer the horizon.

Or try different types of wave patterns, like these, for a choppier sea.

Palm tree tricks

1 Use felt-tip pens to draw the trunk and branches.
2 Pencil in the leaf shapes. Fill in the details with felt-tip pen.
3 Erase any guidelines, color in the trunk and draw lines for bark rings. Add some green grass at the base.

3 Using felt-tip pens, draw some trees on an island. Draw in your boat.

4 Paint the boat's sails white and color the rest. When your painting's finished, peel away the masking tape around the edge.

Quickdraw
...a boat

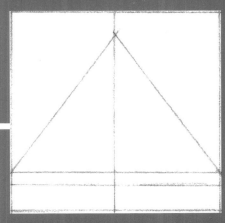

Draw a square with a line down the center. Add another line across the bottom for the deck.

Add a horizontal line above the deck and make it into a large triangle for the sails.

Draw the boat's hull. Finish the sails. Add portholes, a flag and waves. Erase any guidelines.

DRAWING ✓
STENCILLING ✓
PAINTING ✓

Wild strawberries

Roll up for a fruity print of yummy strawberries! They look good enough to eat!

Yum, these look tastier than cheese!

OOPS! To load your roller pour the paint on to several large sheets of newspaper first. This will make it easier to roll the roller in the paint.

What you need:
★ Sheet of Letter size paper ★ Ruler
★ Pencil ★ Scissors
★ Sheets of thin colored paper in blue, purple, red, green, yellow and orange ★ Sheet of thin card (9" x 9")
★ White glue
★ Black felt-tip pen
★ Poster paints in red, blue, yellow, dark green, orange, white and lime green ★ Mini roller (available from hardware stores)
★ Old newspaper
★ Fine and medium paintbrushes
★ Thin cord (5" long)
★ Masking tape

1 From the paper, cut six squares, 2″ x 2″. Copy a strawberry outline on to each one. Cut out the middles to make six strawberry stencils.

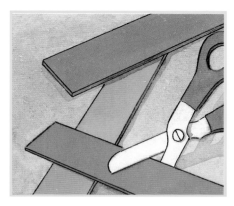

2 From blue paper, cut three rectangles, 2″ x 1″. Repeat with the other papers – to make purple, red, green, yellow and orange rectangles.

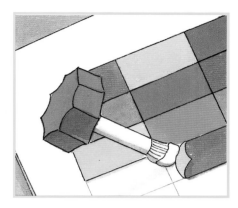

3 Draw a 6″ wide border round the thin card. Divide the middle into 18 rectangles, 2″ x 1″. Then glue down the colored paper rectangles.

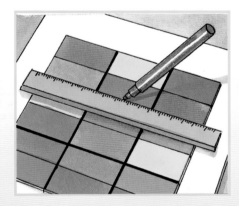

4 Use a black felt-tip pen and a ruler to draw two lines down and two lines across, to turn the rectangles into nine two-color squares.

5 Place a stencil over a square. Roll over the roller, loaded with paint. Repeat, using a fresh stencil every time you change paint color.

6 When the paint is dry, use a black felt-tip pen to draw in the seeds and leaf outlines. Use a fine brush to paint on leaves in contrasting colors.

7 Use a medium brush to paint the border of the card in lime green. Be extra careful not to paint over the colored paper in the middle!

8 When the paint is dry, use a black felt-tip pen to draw a wobbly outline for the frame. Decorate with some fancy swirls. Cut out your frame.

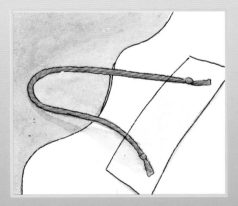

9 Turn over your picture. Take the piece of cord, knot the two ends and tape near to the top to make a loop. Hang – and admire!

Tutti fruity!

Try making some simple stencils for a bowlful of mouth-watering fruits.

Totally tropical!
Make an oval-shaped stencil, crisscross six thin strips of paper over the top, then print. Finish off by stencilling a leaf on the top.

Vine not?
Grapes are easy! Simply stencil a circle over and over. Draw in the woody stalk with black and green felt-tip pens.

Mellow melon
To make a slice of thirst-quenching watermelon, make one stencil of a semicircle (for the red flesh) and another one with a thick curve (for the green skin). Don't forget to add some black seeds with a felt-tip pen!

Cheery cherries
Cut out a cherry-shaped stencil. Print in overlapping pairs, then draw in the stalks.

Have a banana!
Stencil a stretched-out semicircle to make a lovely, fat banana. A few strokes in black felt-tip pen will finish off the details.

FUN FACTS

The strawberry plant belongs to the same family as the rose.

The biggest strawberry ever grown weighed 8 ounces - what a whopper!

Jason Schayot holds a strange world record: spitting a watermelon seed 75 feet! But German Horst Ortmann spat a cherry pit an amazing 95 feet!

Each flower on a pineapple plant only blooms for a day before it develops into a fruitlet, or baby fruit!

Manatee magic

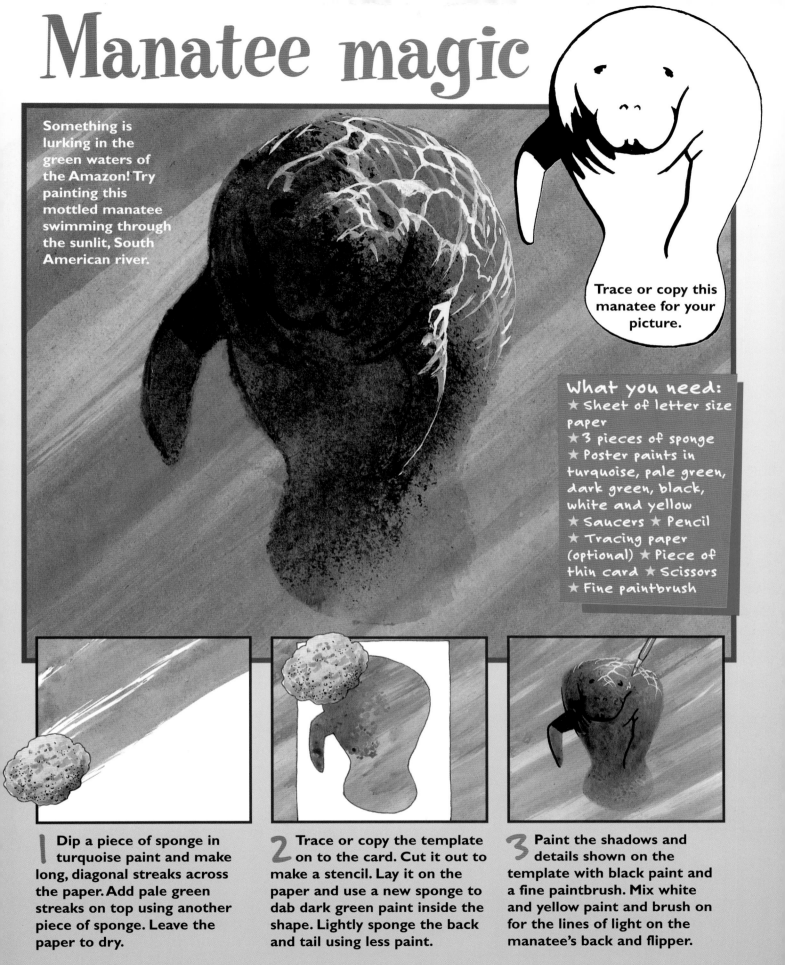

Something is lurking in the green waters of the Amazon! Try painting this mottled manatee swimming through the sunlit, South American river.

Trace or copy this manatee for your picture.

What you need:
★ Sheet of letter size paper
★ 3 pieces of sponge
★ Poster paints in turquoise, pale green, dark green, black, white and yellow
★ Saucers ★ Pencil
★ Tracing paper (optional) ★ Piece of thin card ★ Scissors
★ Fine paintbrush

1 Dip a piece of sponge in turquoise paint and make long, diagonal streaks across the paper. Add pale green streaks on top using another piece of sponge. Leave the paper to dry.

2 Trace or copy the template on to the card. Cut it out to make a stencil. Lay it on the paper and use a new sponge to dab dark green paint inside the shape. Lightly sponge the back and tail using less paint.

3 Paint the shadows and details shown on the template with black paint and a fine paintbrush. Mix white and yellow paint and brush on for the lines of light on the manatee's back and flipper.

COLOR COM

Drag a comb through thick paint to make wild and wonderful patterns! Use an ordinary plastic comb, or try making your own out of stiff card.

You can make lots of interesting patterns using different combs. The patterns will depend on how close together the teeth of the combs are. When you've experimented with an ordinary comb, try using a short comb with wide-spaced teeth, or an old toothbrush with tiny bristles. Forks are good too — try a two-pronged vegetable fork or a plastic fork.

Wide-toothed comb

Long comb

Toothbrush

Vegetable fork

Plastic fork

Making your own comb

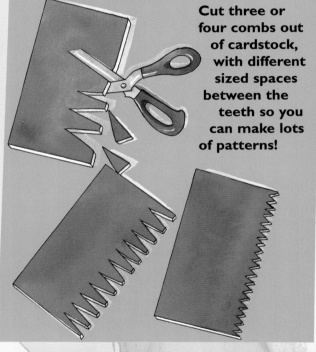

Cut three or four combs out of cardstock, with different sized spaces between the teeth so you can make lots of patterns!

Combing is easy

1

Mix flour and poster paint into a thick paste. Paint bands of color.

2

While the paint is wet, drag different combs through it.

3

You can make circles in the paint with a piece of cardstock.

BING

Combing collage!

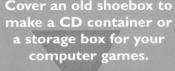

Cut simple shapes from the most exciting areas of your combed patterns.

Arrange the shapes on a piece of cardstock to make an interesting collage, then glue them down.

Cover lots of useful things!

Store your art materials in style! Cover an old coffee can with a strip of combed paper to make a handy holder.

Cover an old shoebox to make a CD container or a storage box for your computer games.

You can use lollipop sticks, pieces of card or pens and pencils – not the pointy ends – to make patterns in your paint. Comb thin lines on top of thick ones for an interesting contrast. Try mixing wallpaper paste with your paint, instead of flour, for a softer effect.

Cut a wacky frame from cardstock. Stick pieces of combed paper on to it to make an exciting collaged surface. Cut a stand from cardstock and tape it to the back of the frame.

17

Color class

Snowy robin

Look who's out in the snow! Learn how to make your own robin, and spatter paint a snowstorm!

ha ha!

What does a bird do when it's ill?

Goes to the doctor for tweetment!

Some people consider a sighting of the robin as one of the first signs of spring! Robins are about 10 inches in length and have an orange-red breast and a gray back. They are easy to spot and plentiful in most areas of the country making them one of the most popular birds in North America. robins are at home whether in the city or in the country - wherever they can find their favorite foods which, of course, includes worms but also high on the list are cherries, grapes and tomatoes.

What you need:

★ Square sheet of white paper ★ Pencil ★ Eraser
★ Poster paints in gray, olive green, red, brown, dark brown, ochre and white ★ Medium and thin paintbrush ★ Saucer
★ Old toothbrush
★ Plastic knife

OOPS! Take care when painting round the robin's legs

STOP! Spatter painting is messy! Wear old clothes, and cover your working area in old newspapers. Or take your picture outside to spatter!

1 First, draw a robin in the center of your paper. For the gate, draw two lines across the page, two diagonal lines underneath and a rectangle in the corner. Draw a layer of snow on the gate.

2 Next, paint the sky gray. Use a medium brush to paint large areas, and a thin brush to fill in the small patches of sky around the robin and gate.

3 Using a medium brush, paint the gate olive green. With a thin brush, paint the robin's bib red and the back and tail brown. Leave the snow on the gate white.

4 Next, paint the legs and beak dark brown and tummy ochre. Paint a gray line down the side of the bib. Add details to the back and tail in dark brown and ochre. Paint the eye. Add gate detail.

5 When your picture is dry, pour a little white paint into a saucer. Dip a toothbrush into the paint. Run a plastic knife forward along the bristles, to spatter paint over your picture.

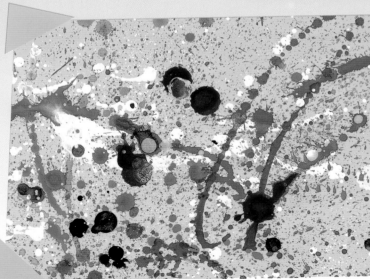

Spatter art

Many artists use spatter painting to make spotty pictures like the one here. They use paints in different colors to build up a pattern of dots and splodges. To make streaks, they just splash paint on to their picture! To create your own spatter art picture, you'll need a large sheet of paper, lots of paints, a toothbrush and large paintbrush. Spatter different colors on to your paper to build up a pattern. To make streaks, just flick a paint-filled brush over the paper!

Spot crazy!

What a lot of spots! Draw your pictures first, then spatter paint over them. Add details, leave to dry and cut them out. Make yourself a whole gallery of spotty paintings!

Spotty boy!

Spotty plant!

Spotty dog!

Spotty lizard!

Who's hiding in this tree? Join the dots to find out!

Quickdraw
...a robin!

Start by drawing an oval for the robin's body.

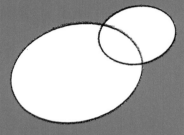

Draw a small oval on one side of the body, for the head.

Now draw two lines from the head to the body to make the neck. Add a triangle for the beak. Then draw the legs, feet, wing and tail.

To finish your robin, draw a semi-circle for his red bib. Draw an eye at the top of the bib. Then add details to the beak and legs.

Brilliant bags!

Make a mini carrier – zigzag style!

What you need:

★ Pencil ★ Sheet of white letter size paper ★ Pipe cleaner ★ White glue ★ Paintbrushes ★ 2 saucers ★ Watercolors in bright pink and orange ★ Eraser ★ Use of an enlargement photocopier ★ Tracing paper ★ Ruler ★ Scissors ★ Glue stick ★ Hole punch ★ 2 pieces of ribbon

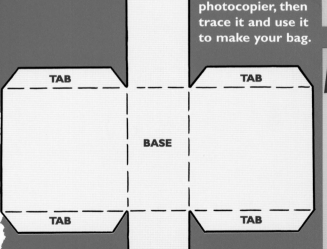

Enlarge this template on a photocopier, then trace it and use it to make your bag.

TAB   TAB

BASE

TAB   TAB

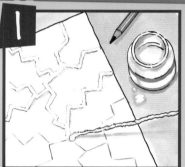

1 Using a pencil, draw a zigzag design on paper. Go over the lines with a pipe cleaner dipped in glue. Leave to dry.

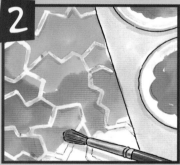

2 Paint in between the glue with bright pink and orange watercolors. Blend the patches of wet color together. Leave it to dry.

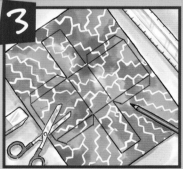

3 Rub away the glue with an eraser. Get an adult to enlarge the template on a photocopier. Trace it on to the zigzag paper. Score along the dotted lines with a pencil and ruler. Cut out.

4 Fold in all the tabs and glue them. Stick the bag together. Punch holes at the top of both sides of the bag. Thread ribbon handles through these and knot on the inside.

All about... BLOW PENS

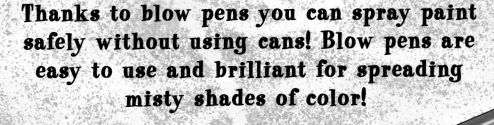

Thanks to blow pens you can spray paint safely without using cans! Blow pens are easy to use and brilliant for spreading misty shades of color!

Y ou can blend, stencil, write, draw and, of course, spray paint with blow pens! Use them on their own, or blow one color over another and watch the colors blend together before your eyes!

Putting it together

1 The 'pen' part of the blow pen is stored inside two lids, one colored and one clear. Remove both lids. Click the tip of the pen securely into the clear lid.

2 Fit the colored lid on the back. Now, you're ready to blow!

3 Hold the blow pen 3–4" away from your paper and blow down the colored lid. Remember — always store your blow pens with the pen tip in the colored lid.

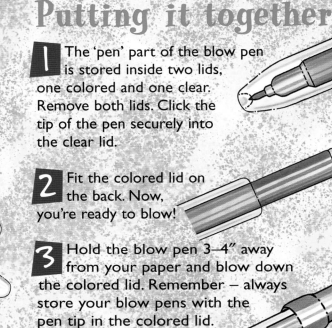

Wow! These pens blow me away!

OOPS! Be careful, blow pen ink can stain, so don't get it on your clothes!

Spots and waves

The first thing you'll need to do with your blow pen is get a bit of practice in.

Draw a line of crosses on a piece of paper and practice your aim.

Now you can aim, try following a flowing line. Draw a wavy line, then spray some curves!

Blow pens ta the hard wo out blendin To blo this beauti rainbow, spray a cur in one color, th follow the line wi anoth

Lovely landscape

Using a coin, a sheet of cardstock and just two blow pens, you can create this stunning sunset.

I could ssspray all day!

1

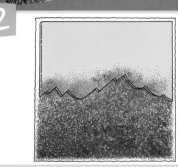

Cut a sheet of thin cardstock to roughly the same width as the sheet of paper you are going to work on. Cut a jagged line across the middle of the card.

2

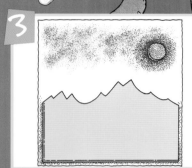

Lay the top piece of card across the top of the paper. Use a blue blow pen to spray mountains. Blend red in at the bottom. Leave the ink to dry.

3

Place the other piece of card over the bottom. Put a coin on the page and blow red over the sky. Blow blue around the coin. Lift off the card and coin.

SUPER SPRAYING

Lay leaves on your paper and use blow pens to blend colors around their edges. Lift them off to reveal fab, leafy patterns!

Clever tricks

Now it's time to get really smart!

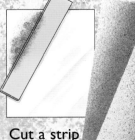

Cut a strip of card and lay it down on a piece of paper. Use a red blow pen to spray along one edge. Move the strip of card a little at a time, in a fan shape, blowing different colored paint along the card's edge each time.

Use objects you find around the house as simple templates. Spray over jar lids, keys and string for some perfectly, pretty patterns!

DRAWING ✓
ROLLER PAINTING ✓
SPONGE PRINTING ✓
STENCILLING ✓

Frog frolics

Roll up! Find out how to make this fantastic, froggy roller picture leap off the page!

What you need:

★ Tracing paper (optional) ★ Pencil ★ Sheet of white cardstock (4" x 4") ★ Scissors ★ Sticky tape ★ Sheet of white cardstock (1½" x 1½") ★ Sheet of white paper (3¾" x 3¾") ★ Mini paint roller ★ 3 saucers ★ Poster paints in orange, blue, purple and green ★ 2 small pieces of sponge ★ Felt-tip pens in black, orange and blue ★ Glue stick ★ Sheet of yellow paper (7" x 7")

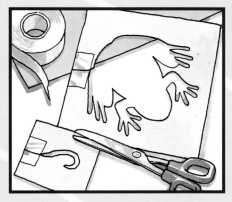

1 Trace or copy the frog onto the large card, and cut it out in one piece. Tape over where you cut into the card. Make a wave-shaped stencil from the smaller card in the same way.

2 Place the frog-shaped stencil on the white paper. Dip your roller in thick orange paint, then roll across the stencil to paint a frog on the paper. Lift up the stencil.

3 When the orange frog is dry, place the card frog shape you cut out exactly on top of it. This will mask the frog. Using the roller lightly, paint a blue background.

4 Remove the card frog shape and leave to dry. Then fold it down the middle. Along the fold, cut out six different-sized shapes for stripes on the frog's back.

5 Open the card frog shape and place it exactly onto the printed frog again. Use a piece of sponge to dab purple paint through the new holes. Then leave to dry.

6 Use a black felt-tip pen to add eyes and nostrils. Glue the picture onto yellow paper. Draw a border with orange and blue pens. Use the wave stencil to sponge on a green pattern.

Quickdraw
...a frog

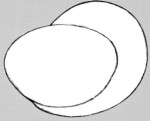

Draw a rough oval for the head and another curve behind for the frog's body.

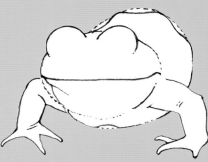

Draw eye bulges and a line for a mouth. Shape the frog's body. Add the front legs.

Draw two nostrils and fill in the eyes. Then, add the back leg and two webbed feet. Show the other foot peeping out around the body.

Draw in the lily pad and cross-hatch the frog's shadow. Add light shading to the frog.

25

Pond life

Cut out stencils to roller paint more water creatures. Use felt-tip pens to add the details.

Lush lilies
Roller paint clumps of oval lily leaves in different sizes. Cut out a lily flower stencil. Roll color onto the points of the petals.

Beetle's beauty tips For this two-tone water boatman, roll orange paint around the edge of the beetle-shaped hole, and dark turquoise over the middle.

Winging it
This dragonfly has a little blue paint rolled over a green body. Color the veins on the wings with a gray felt-tip pen.

Perfect pondskater
Sponge a little brown over this pondskater's green body. Use a brown felt-tip pen for stilt-like legs. Paint the water pale blue.

Shell out!
Even quite blobby, roller-painted shapes can come to life with a few clever felt-tip pen lines. Check out this wobbly water snail.

Cute newt!
Roll green paint for the crested top of a newt, and orange for its underbelly and legs. Add a dark line underneath.

Fine fins
Leave some space around this roller-painted fish shape when you draw your felt-tip pen outline. The white paper background makes the fins and tail!

FUN FACTS

The paradoxical frog becomes smaller as it grows up! As a tadpole, this odd amphibian can reach a length of 10", but the adult frog never grows longer than 3"!

The female common frog lays about 3,500 eggs at a time! Predators such as fish, newts and ducks pick off enough eggs and tadpoles to prevent a plague of frogs.

The female Darwin's frog of South America lays its eggs on moist ground, and the father gobbles them up! He stores the eggs in his throat, keeping them safe from enemies.

Color class

Paint a night owl

What you need:
★ Sheet of letter size paper ★ 2B pencil ★ Eraser ★ Thin and medium paintbrush ★ Poster paints in light brown, dark brown, black, gray, blue and white ★ Fine, black felt-tip pen

Tu-whit, tu-whoo… This owl's come out with the moon! Learn to draw and paint your own owl against a midnight sky.

ha ha!
What goes whit-tu, whoo-tu?
An owl flying backwards!

Owl wings and feathers

To draw an owl wing, start with an oval shape. Inside the oval, on the right side, draw in some finger-shaped feathers. For the other wing, draw the feathers on the left side. Notice how the feathers get smaller under the wing.

Next, draw some tiny feathers in the middle of the wing. Using a thin brush, paint the top half of each feather light brown. Leave to dry, then paint a thin dark brown line along the top of the feathers. To finish your wing, paint dots of dark brown on each feather.

1 At the top of the paper draw an owl. Next, at the side, draw a tree with a branch. Then add a moon and some stars.

2 Using a thin brush, paint the owl's wings, tail and body light and dark brown. Paint the eyes black and the beak gray.

To paint the owl's eyes, use a fine brush and black paint, or a fine, black felt-tip pen. Leave a white dot in the middle. Paint half the beak gray.

OPS!

Take care when you're painting around the owl

3 With a medium brush, paint the sky blue and the tree black. Using a thin brush, paint the moon and stars white.

4 When your picture is dry, use a thin brush to paint a few white lines on the tree, to look like bark.

Use a pencil to shade in the owl's feet and add details. Draw claws in fine, black felt-tip pen.

Tile style

Liven up a plain tile with a pattern of brightly-colored bugs!

What you need:

★ Fine paintbrush
★ Ceramic paints in bright pink, orange, black, red and green
★ White tile ★ Saucer

ha ha! What do you call a nervous insect?

A jitterbug!

oops! Follow the instructions on your ceramic paint to make sure the paint dries properly.

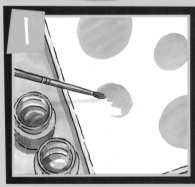

1 Start off by painting seven oval shapes on a clean tile. Use bright pink and orange ceramic paints, making sure the shapes aren't too close together.

2 Now it's time to add some detail! Use black paint to add three legs on either side of each bug. Finish off with two antennae and some eyes.

3 When the paint is completely dry, you can decorate the bugs with the red ceramic paint. Go wild with stripes, squiggles and spiral patterns!

4 Carefully paint a green background around the bugs. When it's dry, add a little black to the green paint and dot on dark green spots.

Color class

A fry up !

Paint over wax outlines and create a tasty looking table mat just like this!

● Wax effect paintings work in a simple way. Draw a picture either with wax crayons or a candle, cover it in watery paint, and like magic you can still see your drawing! That's because wax and water don't mix, so wherever there's wax, your watery paint just slides off!

● Experiment a bit with your paint before you start your actual food mat. Mix a few different strengths of paint, then see which mixture works best when you paint it over the wax lines.

ha ha
How does a fish lay a table?
He uses plaice mats!

What you need:

★ Colored wax crayons or white wax candle
★ 3 Sheets of thin, white cardstock ★ Side plate to draw around
★ Poster paints in red, yellow, pink, brown, blue and green ★ Saucer
★ Paintbrush ★ Scissors
★ White glue or glue stick ★ See-through plastic letter size report cover ★ Colored insulating tape

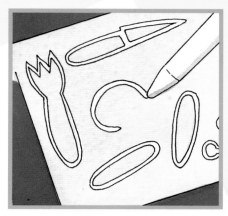

1   With wax crayons or a candle, draw mushrooms, two sausages, a tomato, an egg yolk, a knife and a fork on a piece of cardstock.

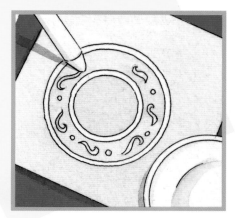

2   On another piece of card, use a crayon or candle to draw round a real plate. Take off the plate and draw a second circle inside the first. Add a swirly pattern round the edge.

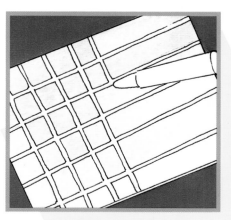

3   To make your mat, on a third piece of card use a crayon or candle to draw a squared pattern. There's no need to use a ruler. Go up to the card edges with your lines.

4   Draw a wax line down the sausages to give them a tasty shine. In a saucer, mix each color with a little water, then paint the food and plate. You can paint outside the lines.

5   Cut out each piece of food, leaving some white around the egg yolk to make it look like a fried egg! Also cut out the plate, the knife and the fork.

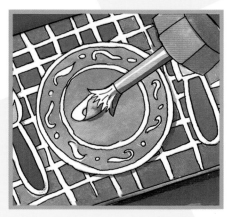

6   Paint the mat green and glue the plate in the center of it. Glue the knife on the right and the fork on the left. Then arrange and glue on the food.

OOPS! Take care of your special table mat and only use it for cold food and drinks, not hot things.

Don't unroll too much tape in one go!

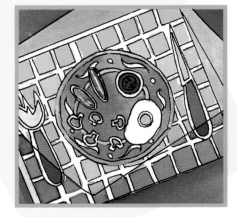

7   Wait for the glue to dry really well, then put the mat inside a see-through report cover.

8   To finish your mat, stick lengths of insulating tape along each edge of the report cover to keep the picture inside.

Color class

Eek! What's in the water?! Learn how to bubble print and make a monster from the deep.

What you need:

★ Poster paints in light blue, dark blue and green ★ 3 saucers
★ Jar of water
★ Dishwashing liquid
★ Paintbrushes for mixing ★ Plastic straw
★ Sheets of thick colored paper in yellow and blue, 13½" x 6"
★ Sheet of thick white paper, 13½" x 6"
★ Scissors ★ Glue
★ Scrap of white paper
★ Black felt-tip pen

The Loch

1 Pour some light blue, dark blue and green paint into separate saucers. Mix a little water and dishwashing liquid into each. Next, with the straw, blow into the paint until it bubbles.

2 Carefully lay the yellow paper over the green bubbles and make a print. Next, print dark blue bubbles on blue paper and light blue bubbles on white paper. Leave to dry.

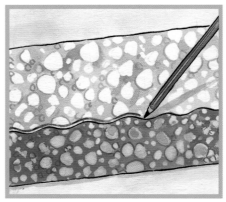

3 For the sky, trim the paper with the light blue print to neaten the edges. For the water, cut a length of dark blue printed paper. Place it on the sky and draw a line along the wavy edge.

Ness Monster

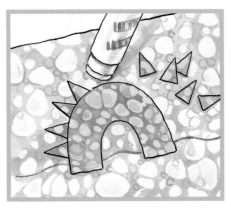

4 Lift up the length of water. Next, use the green bubble print to make your monster. Cut out the head and neck, tail, two arch shapes for the body and small triangles for spikes.

5 Stick the pieces of monster on to the sky, so the bottom of the body, neck and tail all overlap the pencil line. Carefully stick the spike shapes along the top of the monster.

6 To finish your monster, cut out a circle from a scrap of white paper, add a black dot in felt-tip, then glue it on for an eye. Finally, stick the water in place, using the wavy line as a guide.

Monster footprints!

Watch out – there's a monster about! Make your own monster-print trail to stick on books, folders and files, or even on your bedroom wall!

OOPS!

Do you want your bubble print a bit brighter? Just print over it a second time!

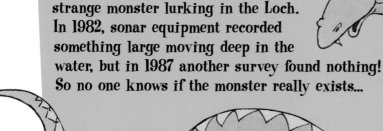

☆ **First, make three or four different multi-colored bubble prints (see right).**

☆ **Next, copy or trace the large footprint outline on to each print. Cut out the footprints and mix up the shapes.**

☆ **Choose a footpad and four toes for each foot-print, and stick a monster trail of them wherever you like!**

FUN FACTS

Loch Ness is the name of a huge lake in Scotland, 21 miles long and over 656 feet deep. For centuries, there have been stories of a strange monster lurking in the Loch. In 1982, sonar equipment recorded something large moving deep in the water, but in 1987 another survey found nothing! So no one knows if the monster really exists...

Bubble fun

It's easy to create your own multicolored bubble prints. Just make one print, leave it to dry then print again in another color. You can make the patterns below using the paint colors next to it.

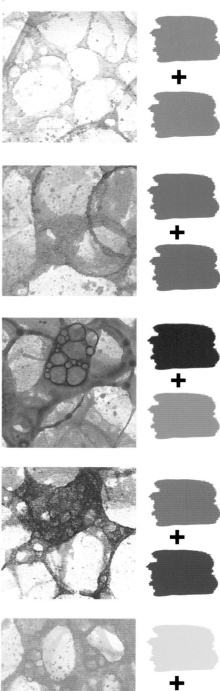

Straw blowing fun

Instead of drinking through a straw, here's a fun idea – blow through it instead! Find out how to get some brilliant paint effects by doing just that.

ha ha!
What kind of tree is always moaning?

An evergroan!

★ Sheet of white paper
★ Medium and thin paintbrush ★ Poster paints in light blue, bright green, dark green, brown and yellow ★ Jar of water ★ Saucer
★ Drinking straw

STOP! For a really brilliant straw blowing tree picture, follow these three tips:

● Mix your paint with plenty of water, so it doesn't dry out too quickly.

● Practice straw blowing first! For the best effects, keep the straw close to the paint when you blow.

● Experiment with some paint blobs on scrap paper – move the straw around and blow at the paint from different angles.

1 On a piece of white paper, use a medium brush to paint in some light blue sky. Next, paint bright green grass below the sky. Leave to dry.

2 Now, using the thin brush, paint in a brown trunk for your tree. Paint in some brown blobs on top of the grass, for bushes on the horizon.

3 While the blobs are wet, quickly blow on them with a straw. Drip paint on the trunk and blow on it for the branches.

4 When the brown paint is dry, paint leaves in bright and dark green on the bushes and tree.

5 Paint a blob of yellow paint for the sun and blow on it to make sunbeams. Blow on some dark green paint to make grass.

Special skills!

● **For the branches,** start with a blob of paint like this.

● **For grass,** start with three blobs of paint and blow to make tufts.

● **For the sun,** paint a shape like this first, then blow on it with your straw.

FUN FACTS

● Giant redwoods, found in the USA, Canada and China, are the tallest trees in the world. They can grow up to 367 feet high - that's taller than 75 people standing on each other's shoulders!

● Sequoias and bristlecone pines, found in the southwest, are the oldest trees in the world. Some are over 6,000 years old - that means they were already 1,500 years old when the Ancient Egyptians started building the Great Pyramid in 2,551 BC!

Trees for all seasons

Start by painting the sky, a tree trunk and blowing on branches. Then follow the steps below and make a tree for each season!

Spring

- First, use the flat side of a thin brush to paint bright green leaves. Leave to dry.
- For the blossom, use the tip of a thin brush to paint on pale and dark pink dots.
- Paint a strip of bright green at the base of the tree. Leave to dry. Blow on some dark green paint to make grass and add dots of yellow paint for flowers.

Summer

- Summer's here and the tree has a lot more leaves. Paint them in dark and bright green.
- Straw blow thick grass under the tree, then add dots of purple and white paint for summer flowers.

Autumn

- For an autumn tree, paint most of the leaves in yellow and orange.
- Paint leaves tumbling off the tree, and a few on the ground.

Winter

- Leave the branches bare for winter.
- Add a few blobs of dark brown paint on the ground, and blow them into twig shapes.

Quickdraw
...with a straw!

When your pictures are dry, use felt-tip pens to add details like eyes and faces.

Once you've gotten used to blowing paint in one color, add other colors to create curious creatures and funny faces!

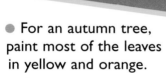

Color class

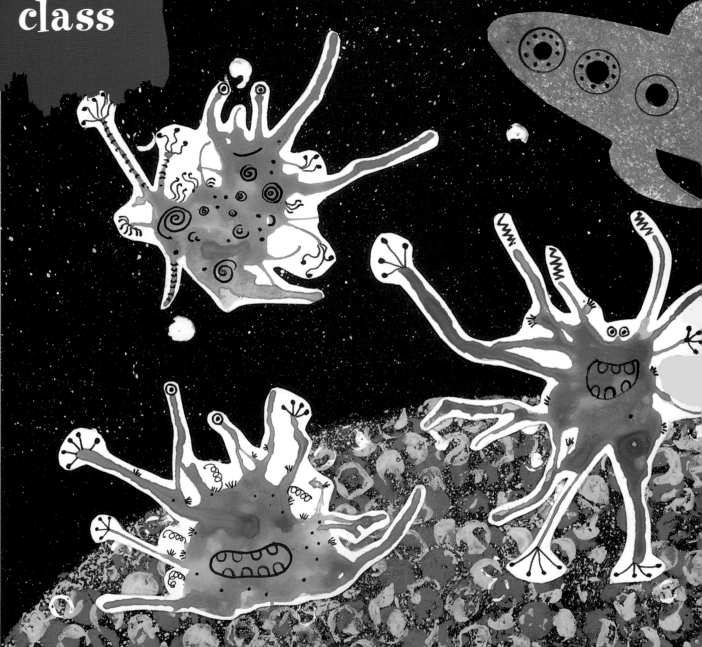

What you need:

* ★ Newspaper ★ Old toothbrush
* ★ Poster paints in white, yellow, red, blue and green ★ Saucers for mixing the paints ★ Sheet of black construction paper ★ Sponge ★ Medium paintbrush ★ Bubble wrap ★ Drinking straw ★ Several sheets of thin cardstock
* ★ Black felt-tip pen ★ Scissors
* ★ White glue

Alien alert!

Travel into space and you'll see that painting without brushes can be out of this world!

1 Cover the table with an old newspaper and wear an old shirt. Dip the toothbrush in white paint. Spatter the black construction paper by running your thumb along the toothbrush's bristles.

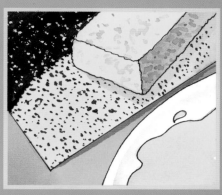

2 Dip your sponge in yellow paint and lightly dab it onto make the surface of the planet. If there's too much paint on the paper, squeeze out the sponge and blot up the excess. Let it dry.

3 Paint the bubble wrap with red paint and press it onto the yellow to create craters. When it's dry, repeat using yellow paint. Add extra planets using the straw dipped in paint.

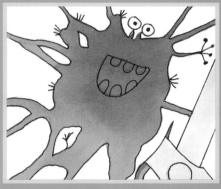

4 For aliens, dip a brush into runny paint and blob onto a white piece of cardstock. Blow through the straw so the paint runs. When dry, cut it out and draw a face and tentacles with a black felt-tip pen.

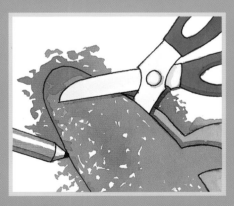

5 Now for the rocket! Wash out your sponge and use it to splodge green paint onto a sheet of white cardstock. Draw the top half of the rocket on top and cut it out.

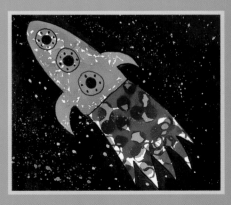

6 Print the red and blue rocket tail with bubble wrap. Cut it out and glue it to the rocket. Finally, draw some windows so that the astronauts can see out!

Put on a cosmic comedy show

Turn your aliens into actors and put them on the stage.

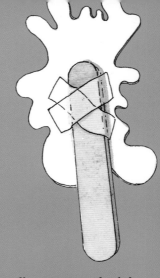

1 To make an alien actor, paint your alien onto thin cardstock following step 4 on page 39. When it's dry, cut it out.

2 Turn the alien over and stick it securely to a popsicle stick with tape. Now you can make some more!

Alien theater

Make an alien theater using an old cereal box. Cut out a window at the front. Paint a space landscape on the inside. Cut thin slits in the bottom to poke your alien actors through.

Phew – that was close!

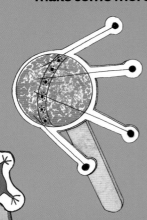

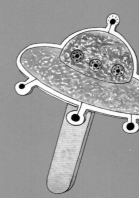

Your alien theater will need props. Sponge paint and cut out some spaceships and satellites. Tape them to popsicle sticks too.

FUN FACTS

🪐 Space dust is falling through the Earth's atmosphere all the time. In fact, if all the dust was collected and weighed it would be heavier than 7,800 African elephants!

🪐 The largest known star is Betelgeuse. It has a diameter 54,876 times larger than the Earth!

🪐 If you want to travel as fast as Concorde without leaving the ground, then the equator is the place to be! That's where the Earth spins as fast as the supersonic plane!

Blob crazy!

You will never lose your place in a book again if you make one of these brilliant alien bookmarks. Follow the steps for making an alien and then glue it to a piece of black cardstock splattered with white paint (see page 19).

FINGER PAINTING

Finger painting and printing is a cool way to get clever with paint. Best of all, everything that you need is right at the end of your arm!

The fun thing about finger painting and printing, is getting your hands in the paint and feeling its texture. Check out the easy recipes below to give your paint a different feel. Leftover paint keeps in the fridge for up to a week.

Get set!

Finger painting and finger printing can be messy, so prepare your work area first. Tape a large sheet of thick paper to your table and keep a bowl of water and a towel nearby for messy hands. Cover up your clothes with an apron or an old shirt. Then, get set to have fun!

OOPS! Finger paint can clog drains. Throw unwanted paint in the garbage, not down the sink.

Pasty paint

In a bowl, mix some acrylic paint with a cup of water and slightly more than a cup of flour. Add the flour a little at a time, stirring it to make a smooth paste. You could try adding salt to your finger paste for a different texture.

Frothy flakes

To make finger paint that stands out, add a cup of soap flakes to some acrylic paint. Then, mix it up with a hand whisk. When the foamy finger paint dries, it feels like velvet.

Lovely lavender

Make the paint smell nice, too. Ask an adult to add a few drops of lavender oil to your paint before you begin. But, never put paint in your mouth!

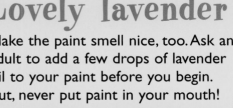

FINGER PRINTING

This printing fun is toe-tally brilliant!

Crazy characters

Print some shapes just using your hand. Then, when the paint is dry, turn them into crazy characters with a felt-tip pen!

Turn a simple finger print into a flower, or even a running bean! A larger thumb print is the ideal shape for this owl and his kooky friend.

The front of your closed fist prints a shape fit for this funny fellow with feelers. Or, press your knuckles down and print a knobbly-saurus.

The segments that appear when you print with your whole finger can make fabulous fish, or fierce and freaky fiends.

Take a look at these guys! Print this kooky bird with the little finger side of your hand. Or, turn a print of the thumb side of your hand upside down and finish off with ferocious teeth. You can even print the Loch Ness monster with your thumb and palm!

Let your imagination go really wild. You decide what to turn your prints into!

Why not mix and match your finger printing and painting to create a colorful scene? Use the pasty paint for grass and then finger print little characters having a whale of a time!

Once you've discovered all the different shapes that you can print with your hand, build up more complicated characters, like this cool crab.

Thumbprint giftwrap!

Print your own giftwrap! Use fluorescent poster paint to thumbprint jaguar markings.

What you need:

☆ Letter size paper in a bright color ☆ Pencil and ruler ☆ Saucer ☆ Fluorescent poster paints in red, blue, purple and orange ☆ Medium paintbrush

ha ha!

Why couldn't the leopard run away from the zoo?

Because he was always being spotted.

1

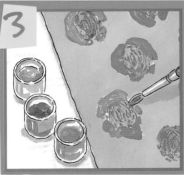

On a big sheet of paper, make a small cross every 2½", so your prints will be evenly spaced. Or you can space them by eye.

2

On a saucer, mix some red paint with a little water. Dip your thumb into the paint. Press firmly onto the paper to make prints.

3

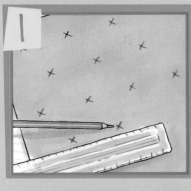

With a medium paintbrush and blue, purple and orange paint, give your thumbprints edges. Let your giftwrap dry.

4

You're ready to wrap! To make matching gift tags, stick some giftwrap onto card. Cut it into tag shapes, then add holes with a hole punch.

Color class

Incr-edible landscape!

You'll need to raid the fridge before you can print this vivid vegetable landscape!

I always eat my greens - that's why I look like a ssstick of celery!

What you need:
★ Corrugated card
★ Poster paints in pale green, pale blue, yellow, white, purple, green, turquoise and gray
★ Paintbrush
★ Sheet of white cardstock (13½" x 13½") ★ Scissors
★ Bubblewrap
★ Vegetable knife
★ Floret of cauliflower or broccoli
★ Mushroom ★ Carrot
★ Stick of celery

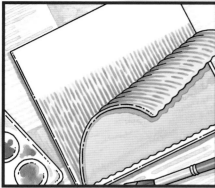

1 Brush pale green paint on a rectangle of corrugated card, slightly larger than letter size. Press it paint-side down at the bottom of the white card. Then, paint a pale blue sky at the top.

2 Let the paint dry. Take a fresh strip of corrugated card and fold the sides up to make handles. Brush on yellow paint and use it to print fields at different angles.

3 Next, cut out a cloud-shaped scrap of bubble-wrap. Brush white paint onto the bumpy side and use to print the three bubbly clouds across the blue sky.

4 Cut the mushroom in half. Dip in purple paint and use it to print three trees. Cut the cauliflower or broccoli floret in half, brush on green paint and use it to print four trees.

5 Cut the carrot in half, then slice down the middle for a triangular printing block. Paint it turquoise, mixing in white towards the bottom. Use it to print trees along the horizon.

6 From the leftover half of carrot, cut a cross section slice. Use this to print a sun with yellow paint. Add seagulls, using a stick of celery dipped in gray paint for each wing.

Tree-time tips...

Print trees in different colors to change the time, the season or the weather in your picture!

Print black tree silhouettes to show the dead of night.

In a bright sunset, trees would look deep red.

Use yellowy greens to make a spring scene.

Browny yellows are perfect for autumn trees.

Brush white on top of green for snow-capped trees.

Two-tone trees in dark green and black will give your picture a stormy feel.

45

Print crazy!

See what else you can find lying around. You'll soon discover a whole treasure trove of exciting printing blocks.

Cool shades
Button prints make funny sunglasses. Draw in the cartoon faces later.

Roll-up, roll-up!
Roll up a strip of corrugated cardstock into a tube and use the end to print a spider's body…
…or a snail's shell. Just add the details with felt-tip pen.

FUN FACTS

The largest carrot ever was grown in Palmer, Alaska in 1998 by John Evans. It weighed a hefty 18 lb., 13 oz - that's one big carrot!

The mushrooms that we pick and eat are only about 10 percent of the total plant. The rest is made up of tiny feeding strands called hyphae, that are hidden underground.

Cabbages, broccoli, cauliflowers and brussel sprouts all came from the same plant, called brassica. Over thousands of years, they have been carefully bred to make the different varieties available today.

Christmas lights!
Make a green print from a conifer twig. Use sticky colored shapes for the stand and decorations.

Fair feathers
Feathers make fantastic prints. Use them to print gorgeous butterfly wings, or flower petals.

Nutty insects!
Nuts and bolts will give a centipede some seriously cool segments. Add felt-tip pen feelers.

Funky pharaoh

Clean up your art! Use powdered laundry detergent to thicken poster paint for this 'phabulous' pharaoh pic!

What you need:

★ Newspaper ★ Poster paints in dark yellow, dark blue, turquoise, black, brown, red, pale blue, white and gold ★ Saucer ★ Powdered laundry detergent ★ Large and medium paintbrushes ★ Sheet of white cardstock (12" x 12") ★ 2B pencil ★ Paint palette ★ Cotton swabs

oops! Let each layer of paint dry before using a new color on top! And don't forget to wash your brushes whenever you change color.

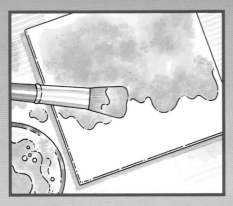

1 Work on top of newspaper. Mix dark yellow paint in a saucer with enough powdered detergent to make it thick and lumpy. Use a large paintbrush to cover the card with this mix.

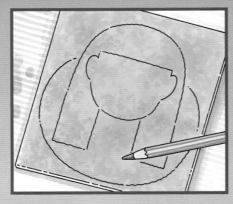

2 Leave the paint to dry completely. Then, use a 2B pencil to copy the simple outline of the pharaoh's face, wig and collar on to the textured yellow background.

3 Paint the bottom half of the background dark blue. Then, paint the pharaoh's collar turquoise and hair black, just down to chin-level. Color his face and neck brown.

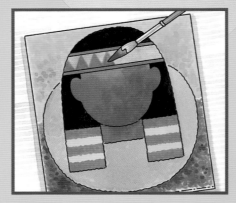

4 Use a medium paintbrush to add red stripy bands to the bottom of the wig. Paint the headband pale blue with a red border. Decorate it with dark blue triangles.

5 Add dark blue patterns to the collar. Start with a circle in the middle, then paint stripes. Paint the facial features with black. Fill in each eye with white before adding pupils.

6 Use sparkly gold paint to add the finishing touches to the pharaoh. Carefully dot it on to the headband and around the collar with a cotton swabs.

Quickdraw
...a mummy

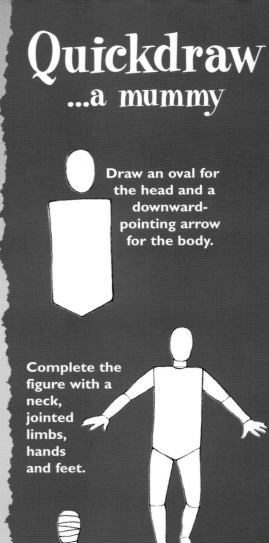

Draw an oval for the head and a downward-pointing arrow for the body.

Complete the figure with a neck, jointed limbs, hands and feet.

Wrap it up! Draw in the bandages. Curved lines on the knees and arms make the mummy look 3-D.

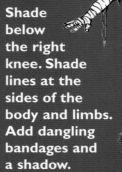

Shade below the right knee. Shade lines at the sides of the body and limbs. Add dangling bandages and a shadow.

Pyramid power

Egyptian artists decorated their pharaohs' tombs with wicked wall paintings. Check out these dynamic designs – then use powdered laundry detergent paint to make some ancient art!

Hip, hip, hooray!

Draw a pudgy Nile hippo and paint it turquoise. Liven it up with orange lotus flowers.

I'm a hippo-critter!

Lush lotus

The lotus flower grew along the banks of the River Nile. This is how an Egyptian artist would have painted it.

Sacred scarab

The Egyptians wore scarab jewelery to protect them from harm. Use blue, turquoise and gold for this scarab beetle.

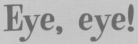

Gritty kitty

The Egyptians loved their cats and even worshipped a cat goddess, Bastet. Use shades of blue for this beautiful cat statue, then add details in black and gold.

Eye, eye!

This is the eye of Horus, Ancient Egyptian god of the sky. You'll need paints in black, gold, red, white and blue for this stunning symbol.

FUN FACTS

- Posh Egyptians shaved their heads to keep cool in the sun, then wore wigs made of real hair. One recipe for Egyptian hair dye included the blood of a cow mixed with crushed tadpoles. Yuck!

- When Egyptians died, they were buried with useful things for the afterlife, such as food, furniture and even servants!

- The Egyptians believed that the sun god, Re, rolled the sun across the sky each day. They considered scarabs, or dung beetles, to be lucky because they too rolled balls – of dung!

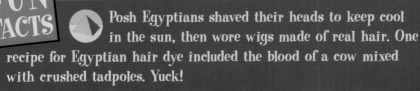

TRACING ✓
DRAWING ✓
PAINTING ✓

Bright Butterfly

Choose your own picture of a butterfly for this project. Look for one with just one or two brilliant colors.

What you need:
★ Butterfly picture
★ Tracing paper
★ HB pencil ★ 2B pencil
★ Sheet of letter size paper ★ Paints in yellow, red, blue, green, black and white ★ Paintbrush

Paint a ssssensational butterfly using shades of just two colors!

ha ha!
What wobbles when it flies?
A jellycopter!

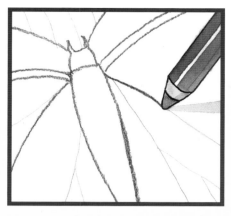

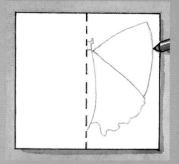

Quickdraw
...a butterfly

1. Place the tracing paper over the butterfly picture you have chosen. Then, using an **HB** pencil, trace over the butterfly outline.

2. To transfer the picture, turn over the tracing paper and draw over the original outline on the other side with the soft **2B** pencil.

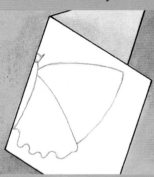

Begin by drawing half a butterfly.

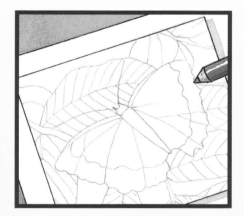

3. Turn over the tracing paper and lay it on the paper. Draw over the lines again with the HB pencil, pressing hard. Put the tracing to one side.

4. Using your 2B pencil again, draw some light, wavy lines all over your butterfly to make patterns on the wings and on the background.

Fold the paper in half, with the drawing outside.

Cut around the butterfly to make a template.

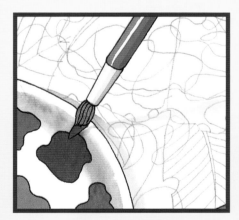

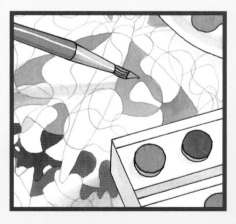

5. Mix the paints to make several different blues and greens for the butterfly's wings. Mix up some other colors for the background.

6. Fill in each of the wavy shapes with a different blue or green, keeping within the shape of the butterfly. Then finally paint in the background.

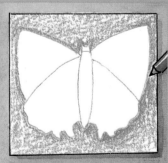

Unfold the template and draw around the edge.

Squiggle pix!

Use the same idea of painting between wavy lines to jazz up some living jewels from the rainforest. Create them with a mosaic of different shades of one color.

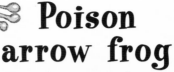

Poison arrow frog

This frog may look scary, but it's so tiny that it can sit comfortably on a penny!

Forest fruits

Many brilliant colored fruits and berries are found in the rainforest.

Green iguana

This giant lizard can grow up to 1.8m long. It spends all day lying very still on the branch of a tree.

FUN FACTS Rainforest

More than half the species of animals and plants on earth live in the rainforest.

The Lar Gibbon monkey swings from arm to arm through the rainforest - sometimes leaping 49 feet in one swing!

Many rainforest caterpillars have stinging spines - if you get stung you can itch for a year!

Rhinoceros beetle

This beetle gets its name from its rhino-like horn!

Giant snail

This is the biggest snail in the world – it's about 8" long!

Color class

Ice cream dream!

ha ha!
where did all the
ice cream go?
A-wafer the
lollydays!

This lipsmacking sundae looks good enough to eat! It was made without using a single paintbrush - well, no ordinary ones anyway! Why not give it a try?

What you need:
★ Sheet of blue letter size paper ★ Pencil
★ Poster paints in white, pale green, pink, pale and bright orange, cream, red, brown, bright green, yellow and purple ★ Saucers for mixing ★ Homemade brushes (see page 54)

Scouring pad brush
Tape a piece of scouring pad around the end of a pencil.

Make three of these.

Twig brush
Tape together three twigs.

Make five of these.

Conifer brush
Trim about six conifer twigs and tape together.

Make one of these.

Ask an adult to cut any twigs you need!

Cotton swab brush
Tape a ball of cotton to the end of a pencil.

Make three of these.

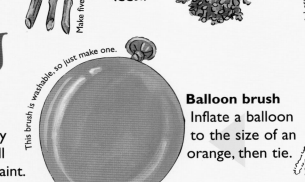

Making
...brushes

Make these special effects brushes for your picture. They don't wash very well, so you'll need one for each color of paint.

This brush is washable, so just make one.

Balloon brush
Inflate a balloon to the size of an orange, then tie.

Pipe cleaner brush
Bend three pipe cleaners in half. Wrap a fourth around the middle.

Make three of these.

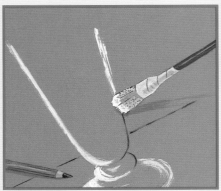

1 On the blue paper, sketch the glass shape. Paint the outline in white with a scouring pad brush. With a second scouring pad brush, paint the tabletop pale green.

2 Dip the balloon in pale green paint and dab on the paper for ice cream. Wash the balloon and repeat with pink paint, and then pale orange.

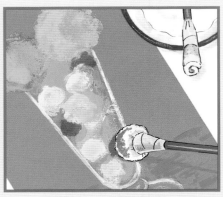

3 Use cotton swab brushes to add the fruit. Paint the pear and peach slices in cream and orange and the cherries and strawberries in bright red.

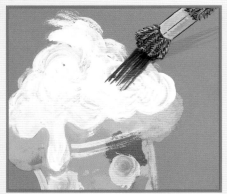

4 Add whipped cream using a pipe cleaner brush dipped in white paint. Scrape on a line of brown paint with a conifer brush for a chocolate flake.

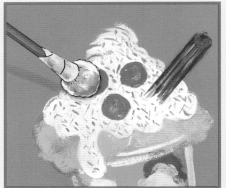

5 Using twig brushes, scratch in sprinkles – one color at a time. Top the sundae with more cherries using a cotton swab brush.

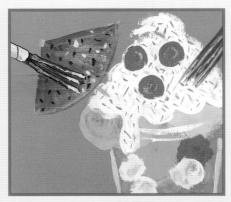

6 Paint the purple umbrella with a scouring pad brush. Add its handle and pattern with a twig brush. Use another twig brush to paint some white highlights.

Scrummy teatime treats!

You can use your special brushes to paint this delicious collection of sweet treats. What's your favorite cake?

Batty for Battenburg
Use scouring pad brushes to make this checkered cake look sticky.

Iced fancies
Use cotton swab brushes for cakes, icing and cherries. To make a fairy cake, add a case: start with a scouring pad brush for the blue background, leave to dry, then add the pattern with twig brushes.

Dotty doughnut
Use cotton swab brushes for the doughnut – and its gooey pink icing. For the white icing sugar and the sprinkles, you'll need some twig brushes.

Swiss slice
You'll need brown, yellow and white paints and three cotton wool brushes to make this chocolate Swiss roll. Dust on the icing sugar with a twig brush.

Yum yum!

FUN FACTS

A record-breaking ice cream sundae was made in Canada in 1988. It had 20.27 tons of ice cream, 4.39 tons of syrup and 537 pounds of topping. Wow! In the same year, some Pennsylvanians made a 4.55 mile long banana split!

The biggest-ever doughnut weighed 1.7 tons. That's heavier than the biggest Clydesdale horse!

In 1990 the tallest cake ever was made. Its 100 tiers stood 101 feet high. Five large giraffes would have to stand on top of one another to lick the topping!

Color class

Go dotty!

What you need:
★ Sheet of white paper (11" × 9½")
★ Pencil ★ Paints or inks in orange, 2 shades of blue, 4 shades of green, 2 shades of purple, pink, red, yellow and turquoise
★ Fine paintbrush

You'll be seeing spots before your eyes by the time you've finished making this brilliant, bridge picture!

1 Sketch the main shapes for your picture – the bridge, its reflection in the water, the lily pads, trees and shrubs. Then, paint the bridge orange.

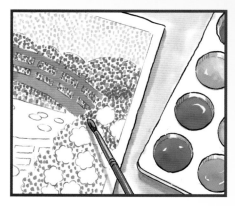

2 Dot pale blue paint over the sky, leaving some white showing. Dot different shades of green over the trees and shrubs. Leave the flowers bare.

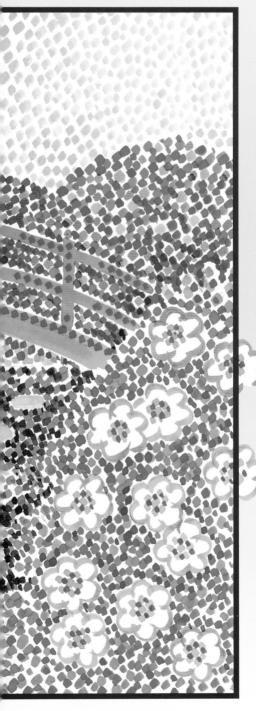

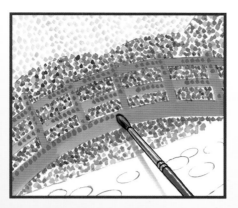

3 Add a few dots of purple and pink to the background trees, in the middle and on the right. With red paint, add dots to highlight the orange bridge.

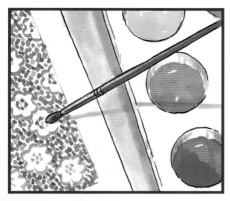

4 With pink paint, outline the flowers on the bush in the right-hand corner. For stamens, paint dots in yellow and red in the center of each flower.

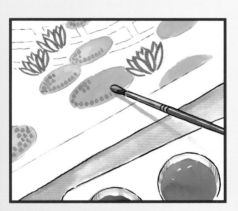

5 Outline the lily flowers in pink. Then, paint the leaves pale green. To make them look round, add a curve of darker green dots to each lily pad.

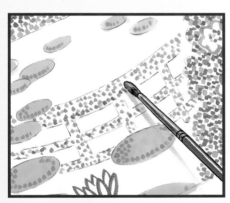

6 Paint the bridge's reflection with orange dots. Add red and blue dots, too. For a watery look, space the red dots further apart than on the real bridge.

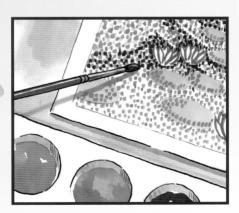

7 Paint the water using dots of turquoise and purple. Go right up to the edges of the lily pads and the reflection. Paint the sky with pale blue dots.

8 Paint purple wavy lines for the willow's branches. Add pale green and purple leaves. Then, paint dark green and purple dots on top of them.

Spots and specks

Try these dotty ideas and see how spots can add texture and depth, or even make your pictures look 3-D.

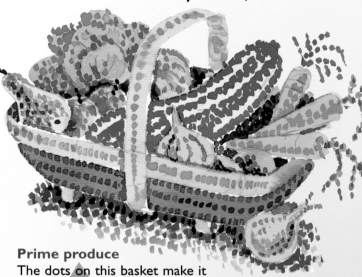

Prime produce
The dots on this basket make it look woven. They also give the vegetables depth and shape.

Mirror image
Dots are ideal for creating a blurred reflection. Try this out.

In the can
Use dark and light dots to show the shading on this watering can. Gray dots look just like sprinkling water.

Autumn leaves
Use dots in shades of red, orange and brown to capture the amazing colors of autumn leaves.

Feely flower
The purple dots on these iris petals make them look very velvety.

Top tomato
Paint dots on top of a solidly painted tomato plant to make the pot and the fruit seem more 3-D.

INKS

When will they make a rat-sized brush?

Inks are used mainly for writing, but they produce brilliant colors too, when you paint with them.

Forget plain old black and blue! Add jewel-like color to your drawings and paintings using inks. You can choose from a whole range of exciting shades. Use them on their own for rich colors, or watered down for a bright, washy look. Try using different tools to paint inks on to your paper and mixing them with other colors.

Dip pens are perfect for drawing lines with ink.

Use a paintbrush for ink washes.

Inks come in all the colors of the rainbow!

Wash it!

You can use water to produce a pale color from a dark ink.

This red ink is very strong. When you use it on its own, it gives a lovely, clear red.

To make pink ink, all you need to do is add a little water. This pink wash is from the same red ink, just watered down.

Dab it!

You can get some great effects by taking ink back off the page too! While the ink wash is still wet, dab it with a ball of cotton. This lifts off a lot of the color and leaves a blotchy effect, like clouds in a colored sky.

Cotton swabs are ideal for dabbing ink.

Lightening and darkening

Lightening ink is easy. You can turn a color into many different shades by gradually adding water. This dark blue has been changed into five paler shades of medium and light blue.

Darkening ink is a little different. You can't just add black, as the ink turns into a muddy color. To keep your colors nice and clear, darken your ink with another color. Orange ink has been added a little at a time, to this yellow.

Snazzy snake

**What's this ssslithering along?
You can learn how to make your
own sensational snake using
paint, ink and lots of water!**

What you need:
★ Sheet of white cardstock (11½" x 11½")
★ Pencil ★ Newspaper ★ Poster paints in red,
green, yellow and purple ★ Fine and medium
paintbrushes ★ Black waterproof ink

ha ha!
Why was the
poisonous snake
worried?
Because he'd just
bitten his lip!

1 Copy the snake design on to the sheet of cardstock. If you want to design your own snake, don't make it too complicated, or too simple with lots of space.

2 Cover your work area with newspaper, then paint your snake and the leaves using the fine brush. Make sure you apply the paint thickly.

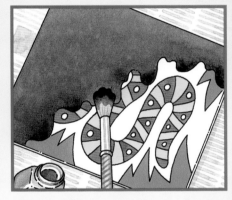

3 Leave the background and the snake's eye, nostrils and spots white. These areas will be filled in by the dark ink. Leave the paint to dry.

4 Be brave! Once your painting is bone dry, brush black, waterproof ink all over your picture using the medium paintbrush.

5 Hold the picture under cool running water and gently wash off the ink using a clean paintbrush. Support the card so it doesn't tear.

6 The ink will wash off the painted areas – and some of the paint will too! Now your picture will be paler and stand out against the background.

OOPS! Make sure you don't get splattered with ink! Wear an apron and roll up your sleeves!

Quickdraw
...a hooded cobra

Begin by drawing long, smooth curves for the snake's neck. Make a tip at the top and work downwards, drawing in the first coil.

Add the bottom coil. Draw a curved line on the neck to show the snake's underside. Draw the head and hood.

Add the eye, nostrils and mouth to the head. Draw stripes on the snake's underside. Create a skin effect with crisscross lines and start shading the bottom part of each scale.

Finish the skin shading. Leave a circle pattern on the hood clear. Heavily shade the underside of the snake so it looks round.

All washed up!

Use this wash-off technique to make all sorts of brilliant pictures. Choose an image to draw, then have fun experimenting with different colored inks.

Summer sailing
Paint the boats in any color you like, but don't forget to leave a white spot on each sail. Then turn it into a watery scene with blue ink.

In the pink
For this exotic flower, use green, yellow and pale pink poster paints. Then cover the whole picture with deep pink ink to make the tiny stamens and the background.

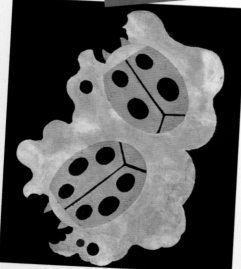

Fishy friends
Leave some white spots or stripes on these fish when you paint them. Cover the picture in dark blue waterproof ink. Paint on extra layers of ink in stripes for a wavy effect.

Lunching ladies
You need red, green and orange poster paints to make these munching ladybugs. Use black ink for their spots and the background.

FUN FACTS There are nearly 3,000 species of snakes, but only about 300 are dangerous to people. One of the deadliest snakes is the Western diamondback rattlesnake, which is from Mexico. It injects a poison, called venom, through two sharp fangs into its prey. Like other rattlesnakes, it uses the rattle on the end of its tail to scare away enemies before going in for the kill - but not always! You have been warned!

Don't get inky with me!

Color class

Salty citrus

Paint this juicy pair of oranges – and add a sprinkling of salt for perfect-looking peel!

What you need:

★ Old newspaper ★ 3 sheets of white letter size paper
★ Inks in orange, green and yellow ★ Large paintbrush
★ Water ★ Salt ★ Roll of tape ★ Pencil
★ Scissors ★ Sheet of blue paper (8" x 6½")
★ Glue stick ★ Felt-tip pens in yellow, orange and blue

1 Cover your work surface with old newspaper. Take a sheet of paper and paint over it with orange ink, using a large paintbrush. You don't need to paint up to the edges.

2 While the orange ink is still wet, sprinkle a thin, even layer of salt all over the paper. This will create a mottled pattern. Place the sheet to one side and leave it to dry.

3 Paint green ink on the second sheet of white paper. Quickly clean your brush and drip on some yellow ink so that it runs into the green. Sprinkle the paper with salt.

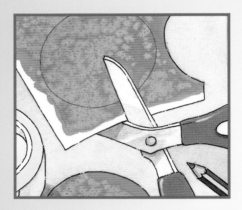

4 When the inky, salty papers are dry, shake off the excess salt. Draw around a roll of tape to make two circles on the orange paper. Carefully cut them out.

5 On a clean sheet of paper, draw three simple blossoms and three buds. On the green paper, draw seven large leaves and three small ones. Cut all of these out.

6 Cover the backs of the two oranges with glue. Then, carefully stick them in the center of the sheet of blue paper, so that the oranges overlap a little.

7 Next, arrange the leaves, flowers and buds on the oranges. When you are happy with your design, glue the leaves down first and the blossoms and buds on top.

8 Use yellow and orange felt-tip pens to draw orange blossom stamens. With a blue felt-tip pen, draw a shadow around one edge of each leaf to make them really stand out.